MARIN BIKE PATHS

A Guide To Easy Rides And Interesting Sights

by
Tacy Dunham

illustrations by
Troy Dunham

Marin County, California

A WORD OF THANKS

To Rosemary Murphy for loaning me essential equipment necessary to explore these bike paths, Dick Murdock for his assistance with fishing information, Dan Sealy for his proofreading and assistance with information for the bike rides on Golden Gate National Recreation Area lands, May E. Ungemach of the Novato Historical Guild, Ashton Hutchins of the Bike Hut in Novato for assistance with equipment and encouragement. Special thanks to my brother, Troy Dunham for the illustrations.

Published by
Cottonwood Press
610 El Arroyo Place
Novato, CA 94949

ISBN 1-877967-05-X

BOOKS BY TACY DUNHAM

Wandering Marin Trails

Marin Headlands Trail Guide

Nature Walks For Children

Discover Marin State Parks

Hiking West Marin

Marin Bike Paths

Sunday Outings In Marin

MARIN COUNTY
CALIFORNIA

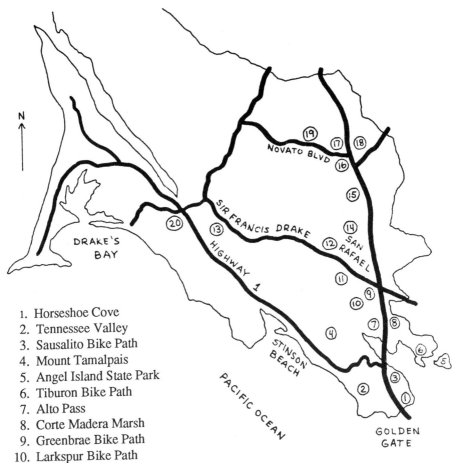

1. Horseshoe Cove
2. Tennessee Valley
3. Sausalito Bike Path
4. Mount Tamalpais
5. Angel Island State Park
6. Tiburon Bike Path
7. Alto Pass
8. Corte Madera Marsh
9. Greenbrae Bike Path
10. Larkspur Bike Path
11. Ross Loop
12. Sleepy Hollow
13. Cross Marin Path
14. Terra Linda Loop
15. Indian Valley
16. South Novato Blvd.
17. "Old Town" Novato Loop
18. Atherton Loop
19. Hicks Valley Road
20. Bear Valley

CONTENTS

SAFE RIDING HINTS

Always ride on the right side of the street to flow with traffic.
Wear a helmet.
Use proper hand signals when turning.
Wear bright color clothes to help car drivers see you.
Don't wear loose clothes that may get caught in the spokes.
Use clips on both pant legs to keep pants away from the chain.
Watch for uneven surfaces, potholes and bumps.
Pass parked cars cautiously, watch for car doors opening or cars pulling out.
Walk your bike across intersections.
Pass walkers carefully.
Have proper storage and straps on the bike to carry gear.
Use a daypack or fanny pack to carry extra clothing.
Carry water and a snack.
Take along a bike lock.
Keep your bike in good working order.

INTRODUCTION

This book provides information about Marin Bike Paths and other bicycle routes in Marin County that are easy rides and offer scenic or interesting sights along the way. Some of these bike rides are on city streets where bike riders must share the road with vehicles. It is recommended that you drive the bike route first and judge whether it is appropriate for the bicycle riders in your group or family.

How to use this Book:

This guide discusses 20 bicycle rides in Marin. Each map shows a recommended ride.

Access:

A street map of the cities of Marin County may be necessary to assist you in locating some of the access points. Parking availability is mentioned.

Distance:

The length of each ride is presented in miles.

Difficulty:

Easy: level or nearly level riding
Mildly strenuous: mostly level with gentle uphill grades
Moderately strenuous: one or more moderately steep grades

Path Description:

Includes detailed street directions and a brief description of the area the path travels through. Scenic views, wildlife and historical points have also been noted.

Disclaimer:

Use of bike paths, bike lanes, city streets and fireroads is at the rider's own risk. The author can not accept liability or legal responsibility for path changes, injuries, damage, loss of direction or time resulting from use of information in this publication. For more information on laws and bicycle regulations contact California Highway Patrol, Marin Office, (415) 924-1100.

BICYCLE ACCESSORIES

Child's Helmet

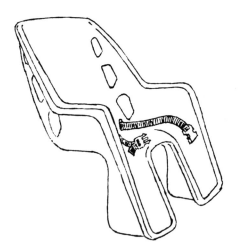

Child's Seat

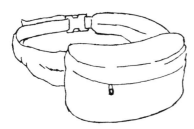

Fanny Pack

Helmet

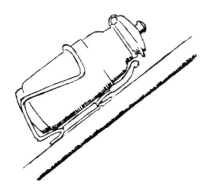

Water Container

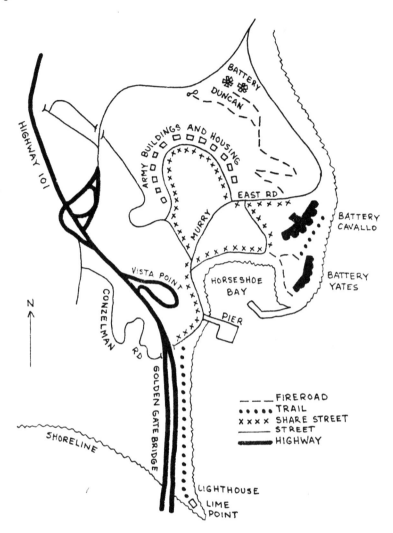

Horseshoe Cove

ACCESS: Conzelman Road, Sausalito

POINTS OF INTEREST: Lighthouse, views, bunkers

DISTANCE & DIFFICULTY: 5 mile loop, easy

SURFACE TYPE: Paved, short section of dirt fireroad

HORSESHOE COVE

PATH DESCRIPTION

Horseshoe Cove is located at the north end of the Golden Gate Bridge in the East Fort Baker section of the Marin Headlands, GGNRA. An easy 3 mile bike ride enables you to explore old gun batteries, see historic buildings and enjoy excellent scenic views.

This land was set aside as the Lime Point Military Reservation in 1850. The original plan was to build a fort similar to San Francisco's Fort Point. The project began with blasting in 1868 to create a shelf for the future fort, but the project was halted. In 1900 a small lighthouse was built on the Lime Point shelf. You may want to begin your exploration of Horseshoe Cove with a walk along the trail to the lighthouse which is almost directly underneath the Golden Gate Bridge. The view of the Bridge overhead and the wind-whipped Gate waters is spectacular from this vantage point.

Horseshoe Bay was the location of the Submarine Mine Depot during World War II. The heavily fortified storage areas dug into the ridge were for mine explosives and also served as mine loading rooms. Today's public fishing pier was the Mine Wharf in the 1940s. Riding around the cove you pass the boat ramp and the Presidio Yacht Club.

Leave the paved street and peddle up the dirt road to examine Battery Yates. This gun battery was built just before 1900 and has a modern appearance. Battery Cavallo was one of the first artillery batteries, built in 1870 with a combination of brick and cement. It is becoming over grown, but its fine brickwork and tunnels are still visable. You may have noticed that the guns at Batteries Yates and Cavallo pointed into San Francisco Bay. They were part of the inner Bay defenses.

Many of the old service buildings, built 1900-1910, are still standing along the road. Turn right on East Road and then left onto the fireroad. At Battery Duncan, high up on the ridge, little remains to be seen except two "fox holes", but the ride up to its view point is worth the effort. From here, you get the best view down onto the center of the fort, renamed Fort Baker in 1897. The historic buildings that circle the parade grounds were built 1900-1905, and served as the Commanding Officer's residence, Officer's Quarters and Post Headquarters. Today most of these buildings are occupied by army families or serve as offices for the Western Region Recruiting Command and the 91st Division (Training).

There is access to the Golden Gate Bridge by riding up the steep, curvy street under the Bridge near Lime Point. Follow the pedestrian undercrossing to Vista Point and then to the Bridge walkway. On weekends bicyclists can ride on the west side of the Bridge.

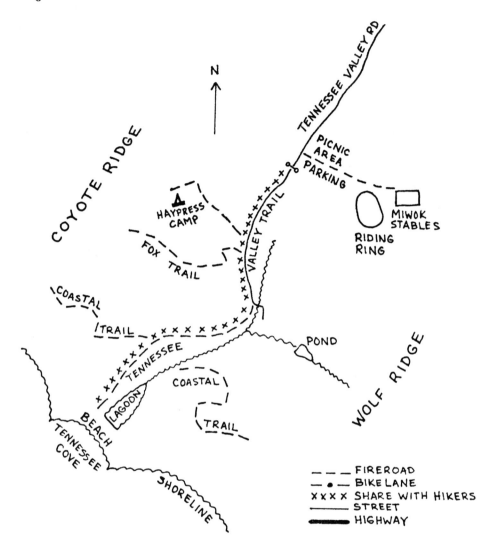

Tennessee Valley

ACCESS: End of Tennessee Valley Road, Mill Valley

POINTS OF INTEREST: Beach, wildflowers, wildlife

DISTANCE & DIFFICULTY: 4 mile round trip, easy

SURFACE TYPE: Part paved, part dirt fireroad

TENNESSEE VALLEY

PATH DESCRIPTION

Tennessee Valley Trail travels 2 miles through a beautiful valley to a small cove and beach framed by tall jagged cliffs. This nearly level trail is one of the most popular outings in the Marin Headlands part of the Golden Gate National Recreation Area. You will probably see lots of hikers and joggers as well as other bicycle riders along the way, so please ride carefully.

The Tennessee Valley Trail begins at the parking lot at the end of Tennessee Valley Road. The trail is a paved street for about the first .8 of a mile and a smooth dirt fireroad the remainder of the journey. At the end of the paved part of the trail you can see one of the old ranches houses which is still a private residence. The barn is where the Park Service horses are stabled. Watch for wildlife as you ride along. Deer are frequently seen feeding among the bushes or near the creek.

The trail follows a stream down a valley squeezed in between Wolf Ridge rising 1029 ft. and Coyote Ridge standing 1031 ft. The creek and seepage areas along the trail produce a variety of wildflowers that begin blooming in late winter and continue through the summer months. Willows crowd into the ravine where the stream flows, creating excellent habitat for birds and small mammals.

This valley has had an interesting history. In 1838 it was part of the original Mexican Land Grant, Rancho Sausalito that was given to William Richardson. Richardon loved hunting and would venture on horseback from his home in Sausalito to this valley known to him as Elk Valley, and hunt the large herd of elk that roamed here. Samuel Throckmorton became owner of this parcel in 1858. Dairy farms occupied the valley until 1937 when it became military property. In 1945 it became part of the Witter Ranch. Witter built the dams that created the lagoon and pond in 1957 to provide water for his cattle. Tennessee Valley became part of the National Park System in 1976.

The area got its name from the shipwreck of the S.S. Tennessee. It was bringing 550 passengers, mail and gold to San Francisco from Panama in 1853 when it ran aground here in heavy fog. All passengers got to shore safely along with the mail and the 14 chests of gold, but the Tennessee was not so lucky. The American-built steamship was not salvaged despite the offer of a handsome reward, and it was eventually destroyed in the heavy surf. In 1981 part of the wreckage was discovered buried in the sand offshore.

Park your bike at the bike rack and enjoy a picnic at the beach or beside the lagoon. The lagoon often has an interesting combination of ducks and waterbirds so you may want to bring along a pair of binoculars. Neither swimming or wading is recommended at Tennessee Beach because of the dangerous surf.

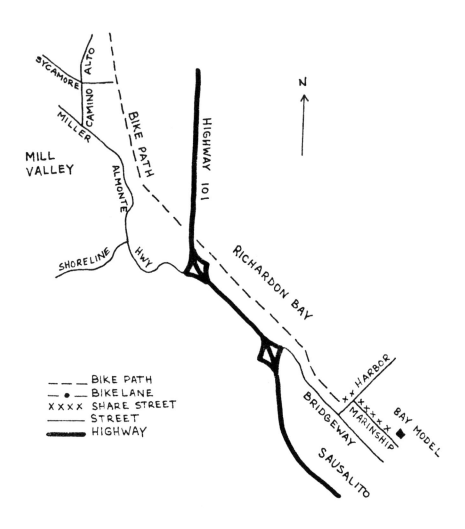

Sausalito Bike Path

ACCESS: Sycamore Avenue, Mill Valley

POINTS OF INTEREST: Views, wildlife, Bay Model

DISTANCE & DIFFICULTY: 6 miles round trip, easy

SURFACE TYPE: Paved

SAUSALITO BIKE PATH

PATH DESCRIPTION

This easy bike ride along Mill Valley's shoreline to Sausalito's Bay Model is both scenic and interesting.

Bayfront Park at the end of Sycamore Ave. in Mill Valley is a good place to begin the ride. Today's bike path is located on the old railroad leeve. From the 1880s through the 1930s trains were a very important part of Marin's development. This railroad line connected with a ferry at the tip of Sausalito and ran through Mill Valley, Corte Madera, Larkspur, Ross to San Anselmo where the tracks junctioned with the San Rafael line.

The large marsh area boardering Richardson Bay is Bothin Marsh, owned by the Marin County Open Space District. If you happen to be riding by at low tide, you will probably see hundreds of shorebirds that come to feed at the mud flats. Shorebirds come in all sizes and shapes. Sandpipers are tiny birds that scurry along the water's edge eating insects. Some of the birds with long legs and long bills are marbled godwits and avocets. They wade and jab their beaks into the mud searching for crabs and other crustaceans. At the edge of the marsh you might see the long legged and long necked egrets and great blue heron.

Across the highway is Marin City. This area sprang to life during World War II as a housing facility for the thousands of workers at the nearby Marinship shipyard on the Sausalito waterfront. Between 1942 and 1945 Marinship built and launched 93 ships. There is a display of old photographs and memorabilia from the Marinship era at the Bay Model.

In 1822 a young British sailor, William Richardson, arrived in California and applied for Mexican citizanship so that he could remain as a permanent resident. In 1838 Captian Richardson was granted 20,000 acres of hilly land that extended from Sausalito to Mill Valley and out to the Pacific Ocean. The land grant was named Rancho Sausalito meaning "place of small willows" for the willow trees that grew near the hillside springs.

At Harbor Street leave the bike path and follow the signs .3 of a mile to the Bay Model. The San Francisco Bay and Delta Model is open to the public, free of charge. This huge facility is maintained by the U.S. Army Corps of Engineers. Many scientific tests and studies on the rise and fall of tides; water currents; mixing of salt and freshwater; and sediment movement are done here. Visitors are allowed to wander through the exhibit area and around the model. Don't be disappointed if the "tides" are not in action the day you visit as they are only activated when a test is in progress. The Bay Model's hours are Summer: Tuesday-Friday 9am-4pm, 10am-6pm on Saturdays, Sundays and holidays. Winter: Tuesdays-Saturday 9am-4pm.

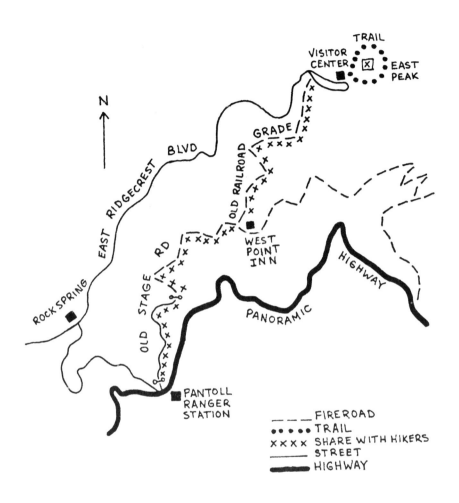

Mount Tamalpais

ACCESS: Panoramic Highway, Mill Valley

POINTS OF INTEREST: Views, wildflowers, West Point Inn

DISTANCE & DIFFICULTY: 8 mile round trip, mildly strenuous

SURFACE TYPE: Dirt fireroad, short section of pavement

MOUNT TAMALPAIS

PATH DESCRIPTION

The views from the top of Mt. Tamalpais are magnificent. The bike ride up to East Peak via the Railroad Grade is both scenic and historic. This 4 mile ride climbs a steady grade, rising 800 ft. in elevation. This very popular route follows dirt fireroads the majority of its length. It takes you to the summit parking area, where you can then enjoy a circular walk around the top or hike up a trail to the peak.

Begin at the Pantoll parking lot, and ride up the Old Stage Road. The first part of this road has been paved for it is currently used as a service road. The Old Stage Road was built in 1902 to provide stage service for passengers on the Scenic Railway who wished to travel to Willow Camp, today's Stinson Beach. The stagecoaches were drawn by teams of 4 or 6 horses and made the roundtrip from West Point to Willow Camp once each day. The Old Stage Road junctions with the Railroad Grade at the West Point Inn.

West Point Inn was built by the railroad in 1904. It served as a lodge and transfer point for train passengers who connected with the stage. The West Point Inn got its name because it stands on the western-most point of the railroad line. Today, the Inn is owned by the Marin Municipal Water District and run by the West Point Inn Association. A small assortment of refreshments may be purchased here. The large front porch is lined with picnic tables. Overnight accommodations can be arranged, reservations are required, call (415) 388-9955.

Follow the Railroad Grade from West Point Inn to the summit. In 1896 the Mount Tamalpais and Muir Woods Railroad was built from Mill Valley to the summit. It traveled 8 miles up the mountain through 281 curves and became known as the "Crookedest Railroad in the World." As you near the top of the mountain, San Francisco, the Golden Gate and the ridges of the Marin Headlands come into view.

The Railroad Grade reaches East Ridgecrest Road a short distance from the summit. Ride cautiously through the parking area to the Visitor Center. During the railroad era, 1896-1929, the Tavern of Tamalpais stood where today's summit parking lot is located. The Tavern provided meals, overnight accommodations and dancing. It burned twice and was rebuilt. The structure stood until 1950. The foundation of the grand old tavern is still visable near the restrooms.

The Verna Dunshee Trail is .7 mile in length and circles the summit providing extensive views out over Marin, San Francisco Bay and neighboring counties. The Gardner Fire Lookout atop the 2571 ft. peak is not open to the public, but you may hike up the steep trail and sit on the rocks beside it. There is a picnic area with tables, restrooms, drinking fountain and a small refreshment stand in a shaded area near the Visitor Center.

14

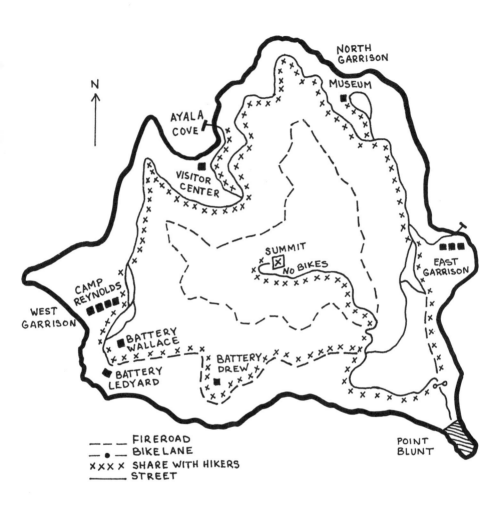

Angel Island State Park

ACCESS: Ferry to Angel Island

POINTS OF INTEREST: Historic buildings, museum, views

DISTANCE & DIFFICULTY: 5 mile loop, easy

SURFACE TYPE: Part paved, part dirt fireroad

ANGEL ISLAND STATE PARK

PATH DESCRIPTION

Angel Island State Park is the perfect place for a family bike ride. This island features fabulous views and a fascinating history. There are old bunkers to explore and small beaches to enjoy. All major sights are accessable to bike riders. Bicycles are allowed on the passenger ferries to Angel Island.

Begin your ride at the Visitor Center. The Perimeter Road circles the island. It is 5 miles in length and its surface is a combination of pavement and smooth dirt. Ayala Cove was the location of the Quarentine Station from 1892-1952 and was known as Hospital Cove. The cove was renamed in honor of Spanish Lt. Juan Manuel de Ayala who sailed into San Francisco Bay in 1775. It was Ayala who conducted the first thorough exploration of San Francisco Bay.

Heading south on your circle of the island you come to Camp Reynolds, later renamed West Garrison of Ft. McDowell. In 1864, during the Civil War, cannon were placed on Angel Island. These artillery troops were housed at Camp Reynolds. Today, the red brick hospital, the row of officers houses, bakery, blacksmith shop, chapel and storehouse still stand. The Camp Reynolds and Alcatraz artillery units participated in the nation's Centennial Celebration on July 4, 1876. A bombardment and planned sinking of a target ship anchored in the Bay was scheduled to be a highlight of the festivities. The artillery units fired for hours and to the embarrassment of everyone, not one cannon ball hit the target.

Continuing on around the island, you will pass the massive cement structures of Batteries Wallace, Ledyard and Drew. These three Batteries were built in 1900. Today, they are partially hidden by vegetation. You will pass a dirt road that heads down, it goes to Perle's Beach. About 1 mile further on the Perimeter Road you come to a junction. If you want to walk up to the summit of Mt. Livermore, take the paved road that heads up. The view from the 782 ft. mountain top is breathtaking.

East Garrison is a ghost town of abandoned buildings. It began as a Detention Camp in 1898 for troops returning from the Spanish-American War. By 1911 it was transformed into a large military induction center. An average of 30,000 men a year passed through this facility. North Garrison is where the Immigration Detention Center was located between 1910-1940. 170,000 immigrants passed through this "Ellis Island of the West" during those years. After the Immigration Station closed, some of the buildings were used to hold World War II prisoners-of-war. The Museum is open March-October 11am-4pm Saturdays, Sundays and holidays.

You may want to begin your Angel Island adventure with an additional 3 mile bike ride from the free parking lot at Blackie's Pasture. Allow at least 30 minutes, see the description of the Tiburon Bike Path page 16.

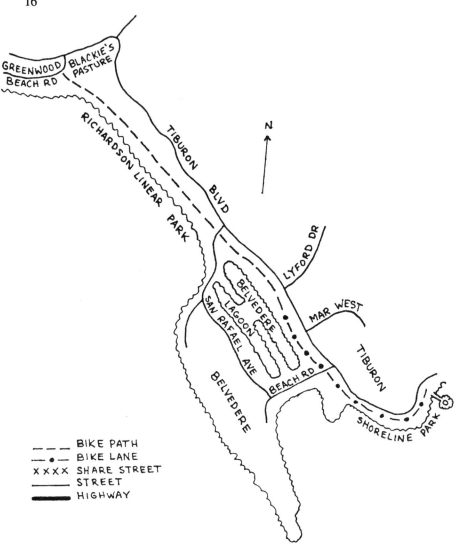

Tiburon Bike Path

ACCESS: Greenwood Beach Road, Tiburon

POINTS OF INTEREST: Bay views

DISTANCE & DIFFICULTY: 6 mile round trip, easy

SURFACE TYPE: Paved

TIBURON BIKE PATH

PATH DESCRIPTION

This level paved path travels along the edge of Richardson Bay and features very fine views of Mt. Tamalpais, Sausalito, Angel Island and San Francisco Bay.

In the 1970s the Richardson Bay Lineal Park was created on land that consisted mostly of old railroad right-of-way. Today, the Park includes the bike path, a parcourse, grass playing fields, a playground and a parking area in the pasture where Blackie the Swayback Horse lived for 25 years. Begin your bike ride at Blackie's Pasture. You may want to visit Blackie's grave site, located in the field, surrounded by a white picket fence.

Richardson Bay's calm, shallow waters were well known to sailors. Early sailing ships frequently dashed through the windy conditions at the Golden Gate to seek refuge in Richardson Bay's sheltered waters. When Spanish mariner Juan Manual de Ayala brought his ship the San Carlos through the Golden Gate on the first official voyage into San Francisco Bay in 1775, his first anchorage was at the mouth of Richardson Bay. During the years around 1825 so many whaling vessels anchored in this Bay, that it became known as Whalers Harbor. It was later named Richardson Bay for Captain William Antony Richardson who was awarded the Rancho Sausalito land grant in 1838.

The Tiburon Penninsula was named by the Spanish, Punta llamada del Tiburon, meaning shark point. The town of Tiburon was established in 1884, the same year the San Francisco and North Pacific Railroad laid tracks from the tip of the penninsula to Mill Valley where they joined the main rail line. A ferry carrying passengers and freight ran regularly between San Francisco and Tiburon until 1909. At that time, passenger service ended, but the train line continued to carry freight until 1967. The abandoned railroad yard in the heart of Tiburon waited more than ten years for development. Today, offices and condominiums stand on the site.

Shoreline Park is a beautifully landscaped strip of land on the very tip of Tiburon. The view from this point overlooking Raccoon Strait and San Francisco Bay is magnificent. On weekends the one mile-wide Raccoon Strait between Angel Island and Tiburon is filled with a variety of boats. From the benches along Shoreline Park you can enjoy watching elegant yachts, small sailboats, speed boats and ferry boats as they etch white lines in the green waters.

The bike route ends at Elephant Rock. This boulder is connected to the Tiburon shore by a footbridge that leads out to a platform built upon the large rock. Elephant Rock is a favorite fishing spot for youngsters. You may want to walk up the road about .4 of a mile to see the picturesque stone tower built by Dr. Benjamin Lyford in the 1880s to commenorate Tiburon's first subdivision.

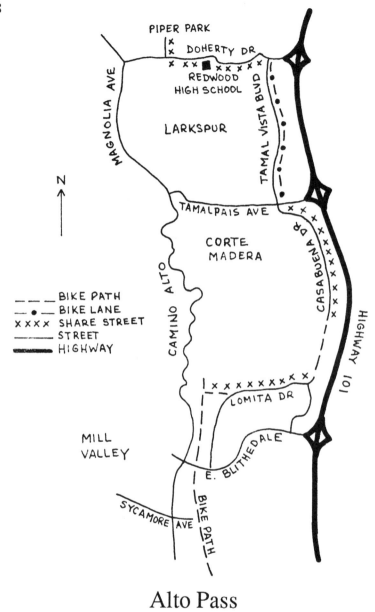

Alto Pass

ACCESS: Sycamore Avenue, Mill Valley

POINTS OF INTEREST: Scenic ride

DISTANCE & DIFFICULTY: 10 mile round trip, mildly strenuous

SURFACE TYPE: Paved

ALTO PASS

PATH DESCRIPTION

This 5 mile ride starts in Mill Valley, journeys over Alto Pass, down through Corte Madera and winds to a nice picnic spot at Piper Park in Larkspur. Much of this ride is on city streets without bike lanes.

There is parking on Sycamore Ave. at Mill Valley's Bayfront Park. Join the bike path and travel north. This paved path follows the old railroad right-of-way established in 1874. Cross East Blithedale at the traffic signal and continue on the bike path. Leave the bike path and follow Lomita Drive as it begins to climb toward Highway 101. At the end of Lomita Drive is the bike path that parallels the Highway and goes over Alto Pass. On the Corte Madera side of the ridge you will peddle along Casa Buena Drive and pass over two small hills. This part of Corte Madera is known as the Meadowsweet area, remembering the days when the Meadowsweet Dairy cattle wandered over these knolls.

As you ride along the flatlands on Tamal Vista Blvd. you have a good view of the lower ridges of Mt. Tamalpais that surround Corte Madera. These wooded ridges gave Corte Madera (which means "cut wood" in Spanish) its name. As early as 1816 the Spanish in the area came to cut wood from these densely forested ridges. By the 1870s loggers had reduced the forests to stumps. Today the forest of redwood and oak trees have returned. These second growth trees are now over one hundred years old.

Just passed the Department of Motor Vehicles on Tamal Vista Blvd. you can see where the old railroad line was. The tracks are gone, but the leeve next to Redwood High School is clearly visable. This branch line split off of the main line at the Baltimore Station in Larkspur and swung out here on a leeve through the marshes and turned north to San Rafael via the San Quentin tunnel. Turn left at Doherty Drive and ride through the Redwood High School parking lot, keeping to the far right. Doherty Drive narrows and has no shoulders as its loops around the High School. Signs direct bicycle riders and pedestrians to use the old street inside the school fence as a safe by-pass, please use it. Rejoin Doherty Drive on the far side of the campus and continue .3 of a mile to Piper Park located behind the Larkspur Police Station.

Partially surrounded by the waters of Corte Madera Creek, beautiful Piper Park has scenic views, picnic tables, tennis courts, drinking fountains, restrooms and a small playground. You may want to bring along a pair of binoculars to get a close-up look at the many ducks and shorebirds that frequent the Creek. The Corte Madera Creek is busy with boat traffic much as it was over 100 years ago. Today the boats are mostly pleasure crafts. In the old days you would have seen supply barges and lumber schooners that docked at Ross Landing, today's College of Marin.

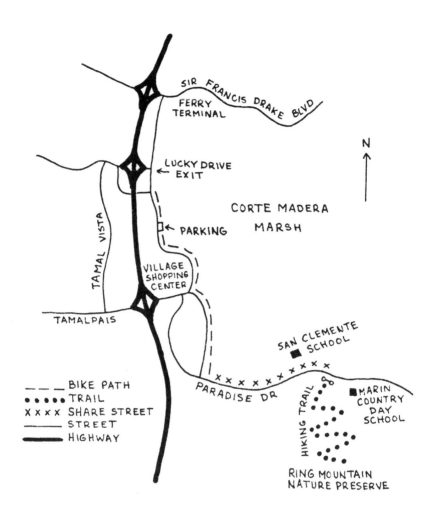

Corte Madera Marsh

ACCESS: Redwood Highway, Corte Madera

POINTS OF INTEREST: Marsh wildlife, views

DISTANCE & DIFFICULTY: 4 mile round trip, easy

SURFACE TYPE: Paved

CORTE MADERA MARSH

PATH DESCRIPTION

This level ride near the edges of San Francisco Bay provides the opportunity to see marsh wildlife, enjoy Bay views and incorporate a wildflower hike on Ring Mountain Preserve.

The marsh along the Corte Madera bayfront near the Village Shopping Center is an ecological preserve. It provides important feeding and nesting areas for birds and ducks. Autumn and spring are especially interesting times to view the marsh because migrating birds and ducks frequently stop-over during their long journeys. This gives the viewer an opportunity to see a variety of birds not native to this area.

Begin your bike ride at the small observation area on Redwood Highway. It has benches and about a half dozen parking spaces. All of the birds and ducks at this marsh are wild, but since the benches were added, some of the mallards have already learned to beg for a hand-out. Join the paved bike path and head south passed the Shopping Center. You are likely to see meadowlarks, great egrets, snowy egrets, avocets, sandpipers, mallards and grebes as you ride along the marsh and slough.

The bike path ends at Paradise Drive and you must ride on the street for about one block while passing the Paradise Shopping Center. Please ride carefully along this section. Then a wide shoulder is available for bicyclists to use for the remaining 1 mile ride to Ring Mountain.

Watch for the Ring Mountain Preserve sign. There is a gate at the entrance where you can lock your bike. The trail is for foot traffic only. This Preserve is owned by the Nature Conservancy. The Phyllis Ellman Trail zigzags up .8 of a mile to the ridgetop. You will see many out croppings of the beautiful green rock, serpentine on this hike. Ring Mountain is well known for its lovely wildflowers that begin their parade of bloom in late winter and display their bright colors and varieties through spring into summer. There are several species of rare wildflowers that live within the Preserve.

Fine views of San Francisco Bay grow better with each step up in elevation. At the summit of the ridge views extend over the crest to San Francisco, Tiburon, Belvedere, Sausalito and all the way around to Mt. Tamalpais, Corte Madera, San Quentin and Richmond. Ancient Indians occupied this area and they left their petroglyphs carved into a large boulder on the ridge top. The curious circular symbols could be as much as 2000 years old. Scientists are still unsure of the meaning of the symbols. In more recent times, 1950, an anti-aircraft military installation was placed on the east knoll of Ring Mountain. The installation has been removed, today only the level area and the service road remain visable. For more information about Ring Mountain Preserve call 927-1230.

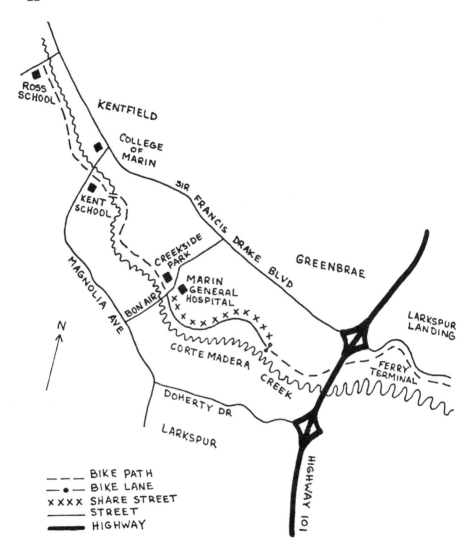

BIKE PATH
BIKE LANE
SHARE STREET
STREET
HIGHWAY

Greenbrae Bike Path

ACCESS: Larkspur Landing, Larkspur

POINTS OF INTEREST: Views, wildlife

DISTANCE & DIFFICULTY: 8 miles round trip, easy

SURFACE TYPE: Paved

GREENBRAE BIKE PATH

PATH DESCRIPTION

The Greenbrae bike path winds along the Corte Madera Creek for 4 miles from Larkspur Landing to the Ross Common. This scenic route is one of the most popular paths for walking, jogging and bike riding in Marin.

Begin your ride at the Larkspur Ferry parking lot. For an additional 1 mile of interesting sight-seeing, head east toward San Quentin. You will pass the old Remillard brick kilns, and a couple freshwater ponds with a large population of ducks and turtles. The area near San Quentin, where the Corte Madera Creek enters San Francisco Bay, is a popular spot for sailboarding. On this part of the ride you also get an excellent close-up view of the Larkspur Ferry boats if they are at the dock.

Peddling along this level, paved path atop the levee you have a wonderful view of Mount Tamalpais and the surrounding ridges. Here the creek is wide and the freshwater drainage mixes with the saltwater of the Bay. You'll probably see many mallard ducks and sea gulls and maybe some white egrets. There are benches placed along the way and an occasional picnic table on this section of the path.

The bike path stops at the end of South Eliseo Drive and you must ride on the street for about half a mile. There is a small hill which is the only non-level part of the entire ride. Traffic on South Eliseo Drive is usually light on the weekends, but always use caution in the area of the Ross Valley Medical buildings as cars sometimes dart in and out of driveways. Cross Bon Air Road at the signal and rejoin the bike path. This section of the path continues along Corte Madera Creek to College of Marin. You pass through the edge of Creekside Park near Marin General Hospital. The Hospital was erected on land made famous by the Bon Air resort hotel, 1880s-1920. The Bon Air was perhaps best known for its swimming pool, said to have been the first pool in Marin.

The Corte Madera Creek narrows and becomes contained within cement walls. This was done in the late 1960s as a flood control measure. Its hard to imagine schooners once sailed up the creek and anchored near here during the 1860s and 1870s. This area was known as Ross Landing. Cross College Ave., ride passed the College of Marin portable office buildings then turn right and go through the parking lot to rejoin the bike path. The College has grown since it opened in 1926 with 85 students and 9 faculty members. Today, it encompasses 77 acres and has a student body of over 6,000.

The last section of the bike path leads directly to the Ross town square called the Ross Common. The post office is still the heart of this small town as there is no mail delivery. Across the street the Ross School has a shady grass area with picnic tables and a drinking fountain.

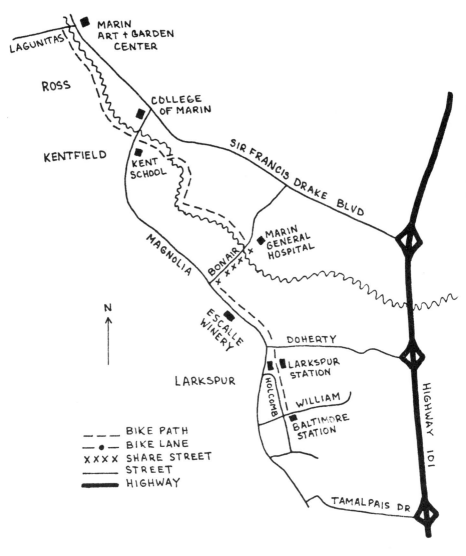

Larkspur Bike Path

ACCESS: William Avenue, Larkspur

POINTS OF INTEREST: Scenic ride, historic buildings

DISTANCE & DIFFICULTY: 7 mile round trip, easy

SURFACE TYPE: Paved

LARKSPUR BIKE PATH

PATH DESCRIPTION

This level bike ride travels passed several historic sites in Larkspur and then journeys along the banks of Corte Madera Creek to the Marin Art & Garden Center.

The Larkspur bike path starts at the intersection of Williams Ave. and Holcomb Street. An interesting addition to this bike ride is a visit to the old Baltimore Electric Booster Plant building built about 1920. It stands about 200 yards east of the bike path entrance. Overgrown, but still impressive to see, this building is all that remains of the Baltimore train station. At this location the railroad tracks divided. The main line went through Larkspur, San Anselmo and on out to Tomales Bay. The branch line ran to San Rafael via the San Quentin tunnel.

As you ride along on the old railroad right-of-way you will pass the site of the Rosebowl, a large outdoor dance pavilion that often attracted 3000 people to its Saturday night dances, 1913-1963. It was located at Cane and Holcomb Streets. Next, you will come to the Larkspur Station. The original wooden buildings were erected on this site in 1891. The train station buildings standing today were built in the 1930s.

When you peddle through a small park at the corner of Magnolia and Doherty Drive, stop for a moment to read the historical marker. It denotes this area as the site of ancient Indian mounds, later a government sawmill, then the site of the Doherty family home and lumberyard. Continuing on the path you'll see the large brick buildings of the Escalle Winery tucked into the hillside. The train made regular stops at the Escalle Station and visitors could enjoy fine wines or stay at the Limerick Inn.

Turn right on Bon Air Road and cross over Corte Madera Creek. Then cross Bon Air Road at the signal and join the Greenbrae bike path for a very scenic ride to College of Marin. Cross College Ave. and pass the campus portable office buildings, then turn right and ride to the very end of the parking lot. There you'll see that the bike path continues beside the creek. This route takes you directly to the Ross Common. Turn right on Lagunitas Road and cross Sir Francis Drake Blvd. at the traffic signal.

Marin Art & Garden Center is a beautiful 10 acre parcel that features walkways and a creek that wanders through the grounds. There are also two outdoor theaters, a pre-schooler's playground, lovely gardens and two historic buildings. The Barn is an indoor theater and the Octagon House is now a library, both structures date back to the days when this was a private estate. The Center's entrance gates are open 9am to 5pm every day. For more information about the shops and the restaurant call 454-5597.

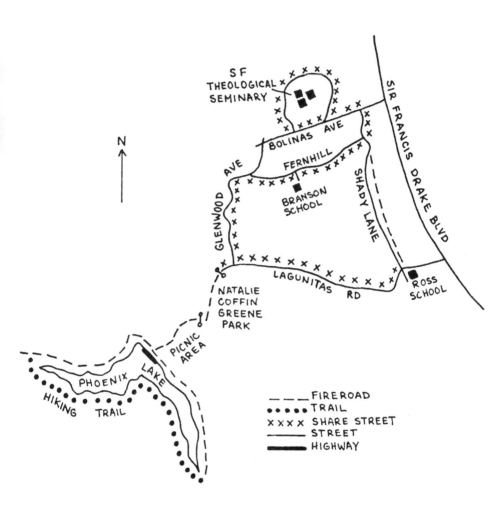

Ross Loop

ACCESS: Bolinas Avenue, Ross

POINTS OF INTEREST: Scenic ride

DISTANCE & DIFFICULTY: 5 mile loop, mildly strenuous

SURFACE TYPE: Paved

ROSS LOOP

PATH DESCRIPTION

This bike ride loops through the beautiful rolling hills of Ross. On this ride you will see some of Marin's finest estates, have an opportunity to explore Phoenix Lake, and get to see the San Francisco Theological Seminary's old stone buildings up close.

Please note that for half of this 5 mile loop bicycle riders must share narrow and winding streets with vehicles. Before you ride this loop, it is recommended that you drive the route first and judge whether it is appropriate for the bike riders in your group or family.

Begin the ride at the San Francisco Theological Seminary on Bolinas Avenue. Take a few minutes to ride around the block that circles the Seminary buildings. The magnificent stone structures of Scott and Montgomery Halls are the two original buildings constructed when the Seminary moved to this location in 1892. Geneva Hall, on the top of the hill, was built in 1952.

Join Shady Lane and enjoy the "country feeling" as you ride along the tree lined lane. Many of the 100 year old trees throughout Ross are elms. Several of the beautiful old trees have been lost to the Dutch Elm Disease and there is much concern over the remaining elm trees along Shady Lane and elsewhere. Ross is a town that takes great pride in its trees. Back in the 1860s this area was extensively logged. Replanting was done by early residents and the first Town Council passed an ordinance protecting trees.

Turn right onto Lagunitas Road and ride up a small grade. Continue to the end of this street, passed the tennis courts. At the entrance gate to Natalie Coffin Greene Park the pavement ends and the road becomes gravel. Follow this gravel road .4 of a mile to the picnic area that has tables beside a creek in a beautiful forest setting. At the parking lot, take the dirt fireroad up to the top of the dam and Phoenix Lake. Bicycles are allowed on the fireroads at Phoenix Lake, and you can ride about half way around the lake on these roads. For many years Phoenix Lake provided drinking water for Marin. Recently, this lake was turned into a warm water fishery for bass.

Back at the entrance gate continue the loop ride by peddling up the hill on Greenfield Road. The street is very narrow along here. You may wish to walk your bicycle for a short distance on this section so that you can sightsee. The estates have beautiful old homes and are surrounded by immaculately landscaped yards. Turn onto Fernhill Road and pass the Katherine Branson School campus. This private high school for girls was established in 1926. Today, the Branson-Mt. Tamalpais School is a coed campus. It occupies part of the Albert Dibblee estate, named Fernhill, built in the 1870s, and was one of the first mansions in Ross.

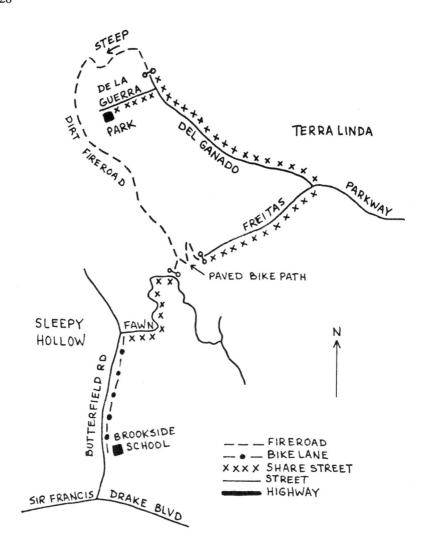

Sleepy Hollow

ACCESS: Butterfield Road, San Anselmo

POINTS OF INTEREST: Scenic ride

DISTANCE & DIFFICULTY: 7 mile round trip, moderately strenuous

SURFACE TYPE: Paved, optional dirt fireroad section

SLEEPY HOLLOW

PATH DESCRIPTION

This adventurous route combines the challenge of cycling over the San Rafael Ridge with a leisurely ride through the two residential communities of Sleepy Hollow and Terra Linda.

Begin the ride at the Brookside School parking lot on Butterfield Road in Sleepy Hollow. At first the bike lane is narrow and the traffic is somewhat heavy, but within the first mile the road widens the the traffic lessens. Turn right on Fawn Drive and follow it as it winds up the ridge passed hillside homes. Back in the days of Mission San Rafael Archangel, founded in 1817, the pass over the ridge was known as Mission Pass. Today, the bike path that connects Sleepy Hollow and Terra Linda is only a few hundred yards in length and it is named the Mission Pass Trail. Watch for the gate that prohibits vehicles from using the bike path.

The Mission Pass Trail emerges at the end of Manuel T. Freitas Parkway in Terra Linda. Coast down the long grade, turn left on Del Ganado and ride passed the Terra Linda Recreation Center. Near the end of Del Ganado turn left and follow De La Guerra Road to Santa Margarita Valley Park. This small park has benches, a playground, drinking fountain and a restroom. Enjoy a few minutes of rest and gather your energy for the ride back.

The Ridge must be crossed on the return trip. At this point you have a choice, you can go back the same route staying on paved streets, or proceed on and complete a loop by riding on a section of moderately steep dirt fireroad. If you choose to proceed on the Open Space fireroad, ride to the very end of Del Ganado. There is a walk-through space on the left end of the gate. Ride or push your bike up the short steep section to the junction of two fireroads, turn left and continue up. Rest frequently, enjoy the fine views and watch for wildlife. Once you reach the crest of the ridge, the fireroad levels out and it will lead you to the junction of the Mission Pass Trail. You may see a moveable electric fence on the Terra Linda side of the ridge. It is a boundary for the sheep that are allowed to graze on the hillside.

Looking east from the ridgetop toward San Francisco Bay, all the land you see was part of a Mexican land grant to Timothy (Don Timoteo) Murphy in 1844. The Ranch was entitled "Rancho San Pedro, Santa Margarita y Las Gallinas." Looking west is the Sleepy Hollow valley. It was the location of a dairy run by Harvey Butterfield, and later by Richard Hotaling. The Hotaling mansion stood at the end of Butterfield Road. It was remodeled in the 1920s and served as the clubhouse for the Sleepy Hollow Golf Club until it was destroyed by fire in 1957. Today, only the grand old stone steps and foundation remain at the entrance to San Domenico School.

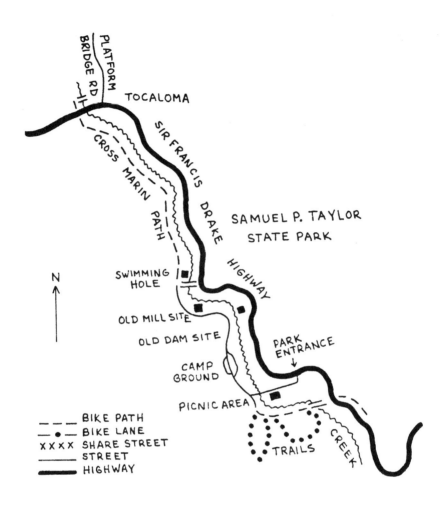

Cross Marin Path

ACCESS: Sir Francis Drake Highway, Olema

POINTS OF INTEREST: Historic sites, wildlife, wildflowers

DISTANCE & DIFFICULTY: 7 mile round trip, easy

SURFACE TYPE: Paved

CROSS MARIN PATH

PATH DESCRIPTION

In 1976 the Cross Marin Path became part of the Pacific Coast Bicentennial Bike Route. This easy 3.5 mile ride from Tocaloma to Samuel P. Taylor State Park is a journey through beautiful oak woodlands and dense redwood forest.

Begin the bike ride at the junction of Sir Francis Drake Highway and Platform Bridge Road, about 4 miles west of the entrance to Samuel P. Taylor State Park. Cross the old bridge and join the paved bike path. You may want to take along a snack as there are many nice spots to stop and enjoy a picnic. Within the State Park boundaries are picnic tables, restrooms, drinking fountains and an old fashioned swimming hole. There are also several nature trails to hike and explore.

The Cross Marin Path follows the railroad grade built in 1879. This railroad line ran from central Marin through Fairfax, and out to Point Reyes Station. The train made West Marin easily accessible. In the late 1880s it became a very popular outing for people from San Francisco to take the ferry across to Marin and ride the train all the way to Camp Taylor or Point Reyes.

Samuel Penfield Taylor settled on this land just after the California gold rush. He built a papermill and a powdermill on the banks of Papermill Creek. The mill employees formed the small community of Taylorville. When the railroad pushed its line through this canyon, Taylor built a resort hotel and created Camp Taylor. Visitors flocked to Camp Taylor to enjoy camping, fishing, swimming and hiking.

As you ride along, the bike path parallels Papermill (Lagunitas) Creek. It is shaded by a mixed forest of oak, alder, buckeye and Douglas fir trees. The forest becomes more dense and dominated by redwood trees as you near the heart of State Park land. Watch for wildlife along the way. Deer are frequently seen grazing and gray squirrels are very active in the trees. The ravines are home to raccoons, skunk, opossum and many other creatures. Many species of birds live in the forest and you may hear woodpeckers hammering at the tree bark high overhead. A winter ride is especially beautiful and interesting. The lush green ferns are at their high point, plus it is the spawning time of the silver salmon and steelhead trout. You can watch the fish as they struggle upstream to find the place of their origin and lay their eggs.

After you cross onto State Park land, begin to look for signs marking the foundation of the old papermill. A little farther along the path is an exhibit with old photographs of the mill and Taylorville. Next you pass the dam site that created a small lake that provided year-round water for the papermill and the campers. The Camp Taylor hotel was located in the middle of the Park's main picnic area. All that remains of the old hotel is the circular cement fish pond which stands among the picnic tables.

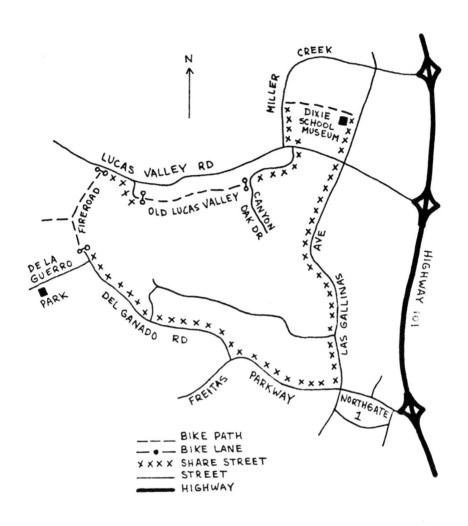

Terra Linda Loop

ACCESS: Manuel T. Freitas Parkway, San Rafael

POINTS OF INTEREST: Wildflowers, Old Dixie Schoolhouse Museum

DISTANCE & DIFFICULTY: 6 mile loop, mildly strenuous

SURFACE TYPE: Paved, short section of dirt fireroad

TERRA LINDA LOOP

PATH DESCRIPTION

This adventurous 6 mile loop passes through three nature areas on its way to visit a community park and the Old Dixie Schoolhouse Museum. The surfaces vary from paved streets to dirt fireroads and you will journey up and over a small ridge.

Begin at the Northgate One Shopping Center located on Manuel T. Freitas Parkway in the Terra Linda section of San Rafael. Ride along the Freitas Parkway and turn onto Del Ganado Road. The traffic diminishes as you ride away from the Shopping Center. Continue on Del Ganado up a slight grade to the gate at the end of the street. There is a walk-through space on the left end of the gate. This land is the San Rafael Ridge Open Space owned by the County. Ride or push your bicycle up the dirt fireroad to the natural saddle in the ridge. The steep section is very short, about .1 of a mile. At the crest follow the fireroad down. It will wind along a creek shaded by bay and buckeye trees. The fireroad emerges next to a small ranch. Remember to close the gate behind you.

You are now at Lucas Valley Road. Follow the street east for a short distance, then jog to the right at a point opposite Mt. Lassen Drive to join the Old Lucas Valley Road which is closed off to motor vehicles. Enjoy this shady ride along Miller Creek over the old pavement. The road cuts along this old street are sprinkled with a rainbow of spring and summer wildflowers. In early spring watch for the dainty white milkmaids and the soft pastel colors of the wild radish plants. By summer the bright red Indian paintbrush, yellow mustard and orange monkey flowers will be in bloom along this section.

As you near the end of Old Lucas Valley Road you will see a large playing field dedicated as Jerry R. Russon Park. The ridge up above this route is part of Mont Marin Open Space owned by the City of San Rafael. A footpath and also a fireroad branch off of Old Lucas Valley Road and go up to the ridgetop.

Cross Lucas Valley Road carefully and ride to the left a short distance to reach the Marinwood Community Park next to the firestation. There is a very nice picnic area here with a drinking fountain. The restroom is near the tennis courts. Continue on the loop ride by crossing the footbridge near the tennis courts. This will lead you through the Miller Creek Middle School campus and directly to the historic Dixie Schoolhouse that was built over 100 years ago. The Schoolhouse is open, free of charge, on Sundays 2-4pm. Be sure to stop by for a visit and see the wonderfully restored building with its old desks and photographs of Dixie students.

Follow Las Gallinas Blvd. south. It will climb up and over an easy grade and take you back to the Northgate One Shopping Center.

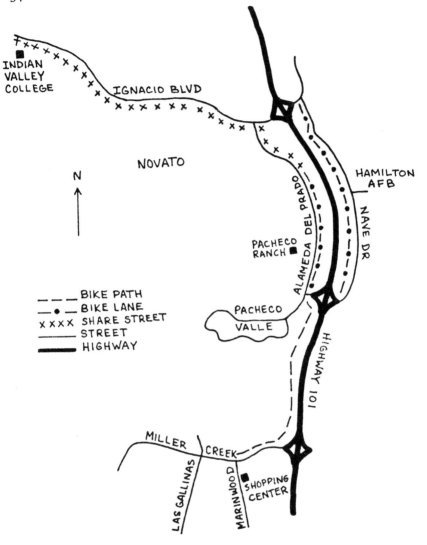

Indian Valley

ACCESS: Miller Creek Road, San Rafael

POINTS OF INTEREST: Scenic ride

DISTANCE & DIFFICULTY: 10 mile round trip, mildly strenuous

SURFACE TYPE: Paved

INDIAN VALLEY

PATH DESCRIPTION

This route journeys from the Marinwood part of San Rafael up over Pacheco Pass and through tree-lined residential streets of the Ignacio section of Novato to Indian Valley College.

The bike ride begins at the Shopping Center on Marinwood Avenue off Miller Creek Road 4 miles north of central San Rafael. Join the bike path that parallels Highway 101 and peddle up the grade and over Pacheco Pass. The land on the other side of the Highway is owned by the St. Vincent School for Boys, which was established in 1855. For many years the school functioned as an orphanage. Today, the school is a residential treatment center and a working ranch. The beautiful chapel, visable from the Highway, was built in 1930.

As you ride along the bike lane on Alameda del Prado you will pass the historic Pacheco Ranch. This area of Novato was part of the 6,600 acre Rancho San Jose land grant given to Ignacio Pacheco in 1840. Pacheco was a sargeant in the Mexican army who became a prominent land owner in early Marin and also served as justice of the peace for San Rafael. Ignacio's adobe hacienda was located near the intersection of Ignacio Blvd. and Alameda del Prado, the site on which the Galli Restaurant stood for many years. Pacheco's hacienda was destroyed by fire in 1916. The large Victorican home at the Pacheco Ranch was built in 1881 by Ignacio's son. Today, grapes cover much of the Pacheco Ranch land.

Turn left on Ignacio Blvd. and follow it the length of the valley. Ignacio Blvd. dead ends at the Indian Valley College campus. This college is the sister campus of College of Marin. It was built in the 1970s to serve north Marin. The buildings are tucked into a beautiful natural stetting of native oak trees with a creek wandering through the campus. There are many picnic tables and benches boarding open grass areas and along the shady creek bank. The ridge above the school and the land beyond the Campus Security building is Indian Valley Open Space land owned by the County.

On the return ride you might want to cross Highway 101, to the east side and peddle along the bike lane on Nave Drive passed Hamilton. The white arch entrance to Hamilton Air Force Base still stands. Hamilton Field was a base for bombers from 1933-1940, and home base for several fighter squadrons during and after World War II. The base continued to expand its facilities an services including the addition of a USAF hospital. Hamilton was well known as the most desirable location for aviation personnel in the United State because of its location in Marin. In 1966 Hamilton was command center of the western states North American Air Defense, NORAD, program. In the 1970s Hamilton Air Force Base became a Reserve and military housing facility.

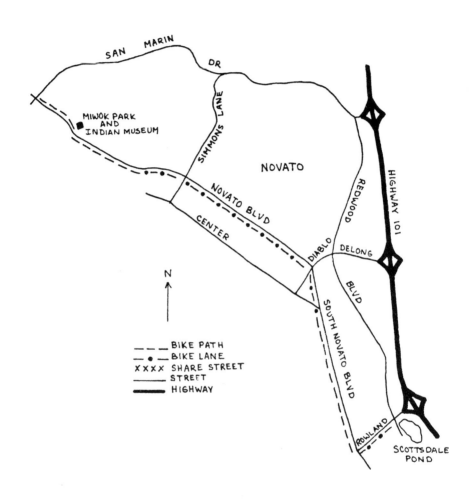

South Novato Blvd.

ACCESS: Rowland Blvd., Novato

POINTS OF INTEREST: Miwok Park, Museum of the American Indian

DISTANCE & DIFFICULTY: 7 mile round trip, easy

SURFACE TYPE: Paved

SOUTH NOVATO BLVD.

PATH DESCRIPTION

This easy bike ride through the heart of Novato's residential area features a visit to Miwok Park and the Museum of the American Indian.

The Scottsdale Pond on the corner of Redwood Blvd. and Rowland Blvd. is a good place to start this bike ride. You may want to bring some bread to feed the many ducks and geese that live at this pond. Turtles also live here, look for them on top of a floating log.

Ride along the bike lane on Rowland Blvd. and cross over to join the bike path that parallels South Novato Blvd. This section of South Novato Blvd. is the original "Old Town" area of Novato, established in the 1850s. Back then, Novato Creek extended to this point and barges were able to serve the early businesses. The first Novato post office was located here from 1856 to 1860. Henry F. Jones was the first postmaster and his home was located on South Novato Blvd. near Yukon Way. The postmaster's home has been preserved. In 1972 it was donated to the City of Novato and moved to 815 Delong Avenue. Today, the Novato History Museum occupies the historic structure.

South Novato Blvd. was the main thoroughfare from the 1850s through the 1930s when the Redwood Highway was built. The Highway passed directly through the center of Novato's downtown area. It was not until the 1970s that Highway 101 was moved to its present location that bypasses the downtown area. Follow the bike lane along South Novato Blvd. and note the name change to Novato Blvd. after you cross the Diablo-Delong Avenue intersection. Join the bike path as it climbs a gentle grade and bumps along over a few bulging tree roots. As you near Miwok Park watch for Eucalyptus Avenue and use the cross-walk here to cross Novato Blvd.

Miwok Park honors the Coast Miwok Indians. The land for the park was set aside in the 1960s when Indian artifacts were found during development of a nearby subdivision. The Museum of the American Indian was created in 1973. It is open to the public, free of charge, Tuesday-Saturday 10am to 4pm and Sundays 12pm to 4pm. The gallery upstairs has a pictorial history exhibit of the local Miwok Indians plus artifacts including baskets, tools, clothing, ceremonial jewelry and musical instruments. A diorama depicts the Indian village setting and life. The reference library downstairs is open to the public by appointment.

Novato Creek meanders through the park. Picnic tables and a playground are situated in the shade of oak and bay trees. There is a hiking path named the Miwok Trail that begins at the footbridge and travels .5 of a mile in a loop around and over the top of a hill adjacent to the park.

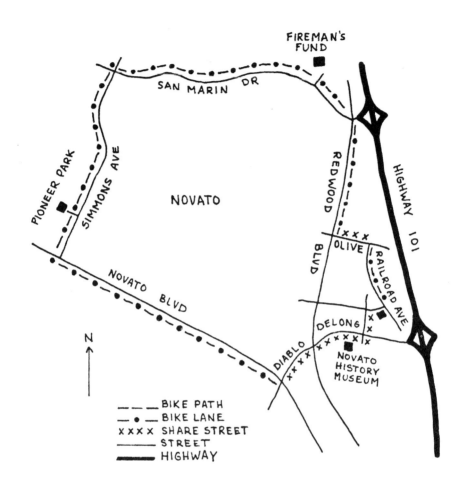

"Old Town" Novato Loop

ACCESS: San Marin Drive, Novato

POINTS OF INTEREST: Pioneer Park, historic buildings

DISTANCE & DIFFICULTY: 5 mile loop, easy

SURFACE TYPE: Paved

"OLD TOWN" NOVATO LOOP

PATH DESCRIPTION

This easy bike ride circles downtown Novato and introduces you to many historic buildings and sites in the "Old Town" section.

Begin the ride at the Fireman's Fund parking lot on San Marin Drive just off Highway 101. You may want to take a short loop around the Fireman's Fund building and see its beautiful fountain. Join the bike lane on San Marin Drive and peddle up a slight grade. Turn left on Simmons Lane and coast down the gentle grade to Pioneer Park. Take a few minutes to explore the Park's 11 acres of grass, shaded picnic areas, tennis courts and playground. On the crest of the small hill is a pioneer family cemetery with some of the headstones dating back to the mid-1800s. The Pioneer Cemetery was restored in 1976 as a bicentennial project.

Turn left on Novato Blvd. and ride along the bike lane. You will need to ride a short distance on Diablo and Delong Avenues which do not have bike lanes. Use caution on this section of the ride as it is on busy streets and crosses two large intersections. Continue up the small hill and stop briefly at City Hall. All the red buildings are owned by the City of Novato. City Hall occupies the old Presbyterian Church that dates back to 1896. The historic Silva-Kuser House, across the street, was built around1900, and the Carlile House on the corner of Delong and Reichert was constructed in 1911.

The Novato History Museum at 815 Delong Avenue is in Novato's first Post-master's house. The house was moved from its original location on South Novato Blvd. to this location in 1972. The Museum is open on Thursdays and Saturdays 10am to 4pm, except on holidays. Inside the restored two-story house is a large collection of old photographs of the town, its early schools and residents. Displays include artifacts and memorabilia of Novato's early days and a room dedicated to Hamilton Air Force Base.

Continue the "Old Town" tour by turning to the left on Reichert Avenue and right on Grant which takes you to the old railroad depot, established in 1879. The depot buildings standing today were built in 1917 and served the passenger trains until they stopped operation in 1959. The train served many purposes including trans-porting Novato's teen age students to San Rafael High School. Novato didn't get its own High School until 1960. In recent years the city of Novato has grown a great deal. The name "Old Town" is used to designate the stores and homes on the east side of Redwood Blvd. near the old railroad depot.

To complete the loop ride, follow Railroad Avenue turn left on Olive Avenue and right onto Redwood Blvd. and ride on the bike lane up the grade and back to the Fireman's Fund parking lot.

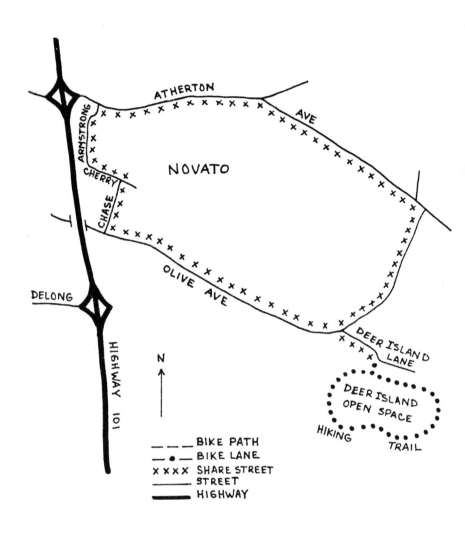

Atherton Loop

ACCESS: Atherton Avenue, Novato

POINTS OF INTEREST: Scenic ride

DISTANCE & DIFFICULTY: 5 mile loop, easy

SURFACE TYPE: Paved

ATHERTON LOOP

PATH DESCRIPTION

Sheep, horses, cows and llamas highlight this easy 5 mile ride through the gently rolling countryside of east Novato. Please note that there are no bike lanes on this loop. Bicycle riders must share the city streets and narrow country roads with automobiles. The weekend traffic, however, is usually light and sight distance is good.

Take the Atherton Avenue Exit from Highway 101 about 1 mile north of central Novato. There are a couple small commuter parking lots on Atherton Avenue near the Highway interchange and this is a good place to begin the bike ride. Immediately you leave city life behind and enter an area of country estates with acreage surrounding each home. This is a popular area for horses and there many corrals with beautiful steeds feeding contently. A few cows and sheep grazing in the pastures along the way add to the pastorial feeling. It is a pleasant surprise to see a couple llamas peering over the fence at you as you peddle by.

The road climbs and descends slight grades several times along the loop. The beautiful rolling hillsides are typical Marin County landscape with oak trees and wild grasses. Hawks frequently sit on power lines watching for ground squirrels and rabbits. American kestrels, tiny members of the hawk family, often sit on wire fences or posts scanning the grass areas with their excellent vision, in search of mice, lizards and snakes. High overhead are the black silhouettes of turkey vultures soaring and riding the warm air thermals which swirl above the hills.

Turn right onto Olive Avenue and after about a mile turn left on Deer Island Lane. Deer Island is owned by the Marin County Open Space District. You can lock your bicycle in the small dirt parking area near the trailhead. There is a 1.8 mile hiking trail that circles the island and a second trail that leads to the crest of the hill. This Open Space land is a nice spot for a rest, a picnic or a hike. Please note there are no picnic tables, restrooms or drinking fountains on Deer Island. There are fine views from the footpath out over the lowland marshes that serve as a flood plain for Novato Creek. During the second half of the 1800s, sloops sailed up Novato Creek to the Sonoma Road (today's South Novato Blvd.) where the very first Novato homes and businesses were established. In spring the island is brilliant with colorful wildflowers. During the summer you can cool yourself under the old oaks and bay trees and perhaps get a glimpse of some of the wildlife that make their home on the island.

To complete your loop ride, rejoin Olive Avenue by turning left onto it and riding west toward downtown Novato. Turn right on Chase Street then left on Cherry Street and right on Armstrong Avenue. The steepest grade on the entire ride is a small hill just at the end of Armstrong Avenue where it junctions with Atherton Avenue.

42

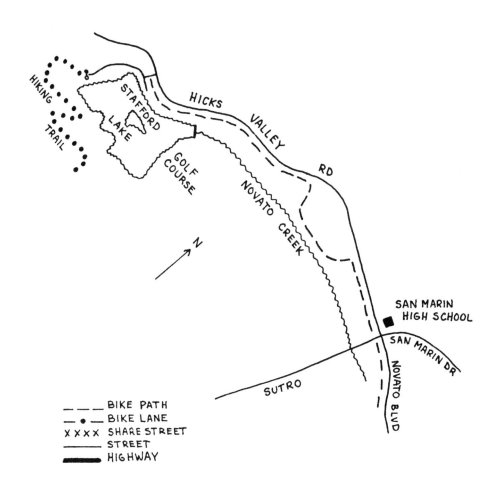

Hicks Valley Road

ACCESS: Hicks Valley Road, Novato

POINTS OF INTEREST: Stafford Lake, wildlife

DISTANCE & DIFFICULTY: 6 mile round trip, mildly strenuous

SURFACE TYPE: Paved

HICKS VALLEY ROAD

PATH DESCRIPTION

The three mile ride from San Marin High School to Stafford Lake Park is through undeveloped countryside. The paved path is level for the first half of the distance then it climbs up a long grade to the dam at the top of the hill.

A good starting point for this ride is San Marin High School at the west end of San Marin Drive in Novato. As you ride along through the valley the path veers away from Hicks Valley Road and loops over near Novato Creek. The creek banks are lined with bay and oak trees that provide homes for a large population of gray tree squirrels. A separate species of squirrel, the ground squirrel, inhabits the grassy field next to the creek. If you hear a sharp whistle, scan the field for a ground squirrel standing on its hind legs emitting the warning call. The signal might be warning the other ground squirrels of your approach or perhaps a hawk is circling overhead. The squirrels will dash to their burrows upon hearing the warning call. These squirrels live underground in a system of tunnels with chambers for sleeping and food storage.

The earthen dam comes into sight as you peddle up the grade. Stafford Lake is owned by the North Marin County Water District and is part of the County's water supply. Swimming, wading and boating are prohibited. The Lake is named in honor of Dr. Charles Stafford who was a Novato Veterinarian for many years. He also was a water district board member who worked for the development of the lake. The Park adjacent to the Lake has a lovely grass picnic area with trees for shade, restrooms and drinking fountains. There is a special group picnic area with cooking and eating facilities, plus softball, volleyball and horseshoe throwing area.

A Nature Trail begins at the end of the group picnic area parking lot. This trail wanders through a freshwater marsh, then zigzags up a hill through oak woodlands to an observation point with a fine view out over Stafford Lake and the Novato hills. Fishing is allowed along the two miles of shoreline. The Lake is stocked with red earred sunfish and large mouth bass.

A wide variety of wildlife live in the immediate area and depend on the Lake for water and food. Raccoons patrol the water's edge for their favorite food, crayfish. Crayfish look like tiny lobsters and they are easily seen as they walk along the shallow bottom. The mud along the shoreline is often covered with animal and bird tracks. You probably will see deer, raccoon, skunk, opossum and dog prints. You might even see a fox or bobcat track. Deer often come to the Lake to drink just after sunset. Many shorebirds, ducks and sea gulls come to the Lake to feed on tiny clams, crayfish, snails and insects. Overhead you probably will see red-tail hawks and turkey vultures. In the late afternoon you may see deer grazing in the shadows on the hillside.

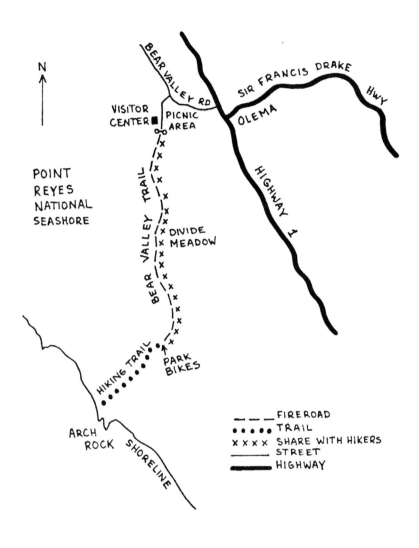

Bear Valley

ACCESS: Bear Valley Road, Point Reyes

POINTS OF INTEREST: Wildlife, wildflowers, ocean views

DISTANCE & DIFFICULTY: 9 mile round trip, easy

SURFACE TYPE: Dirt fireroad

BEAR VALLEY

PATH DESCRIPTION

The Bear Valley Trail is probably the most popular path for hiking and bike riding on the Point Reyes National Seashore. You will pass through deep forest with a creek trickling alongside the trail and emerge at the coast to see fantastic ocean views at Arch Rock.

Be sure to begin your visit to the National Seashore at the Bear Valley Visitor Center. Inside you will find excellent exhibits which include natural history dioramas, pictorial history displays and artifacts from the local Indians, explorers and shipwrecks. There are various slide presentations plus an introductory film, and a working seismograph for you to see.

The Bear Valley Trail begins at the end of the Visitor Center parking lot. This trail journeys 4.5 miles to the ocean at Arch Rock. Bicycles, however, are only allowed on the fireroad section of the trail which is 3.3 miles in length. Bike riders must leave their bicycles at the bike rack and walk the remaining .8 of a mile which is for foot traffic only. The bike ride is easy along the smooth dirt fireroad which has only a couple of slight grades on the entire route. The final .8 of a mile to Arch Rock is an easy walk and is highly recommended.

The delightful trek along the Bear Valley Trail to the ocean follows two creeks through thick forest. As you ride along the creek to Divide Meadow you will notice that the stream flows toward the Bear Valley Visitor Center to empty into Tomales Bay. After Divide Meadow the creek flows toward the ocean, hense the name for the meadow.

Divide Meadow was the site of a hunting lodge back in the early 1900s. The wilderness that surrounded the hunting lodge was plentiful with big game animals including mountain lions, bear, elk and deer. Today, Divide Meadow is a picnic area with tables and is a lovely spot for a rest or snack. You might see the locally common black-tail deer browsing around the edges of the grass area. The non-native white Fallow Deer are sometimes seen in this area. They were bred in Europe for their white color and introduced here in the 1930s. The rarely seen Axis Deer is also non-native. They have spots on their backs as adults and live deep in the woods.

As you walk the last .8 of a mile to the ocean, you will emerge from the forest and cross the open grassland which lines the coast. There aren't any picnic tables or facilities at Arch Rock. Just sit down anywhere and let the fabulous view of the Marin County coastline spread out before you. If it is a clear day, you will be able to see across Drake's Bay to the Point Reyes Head. The Farallon Islands, 26 miles out to sea, may be visable on the horizon. Down at the water's edge is a natural arch that was carved out by the waves.

CALIFORNIA BICYCLE LAWS

RIGHTS AND RESPONSIBILITIES

Every person riding a bicycle upon a roadway or any paved shoulder has all the rights and is subject to all the duties applicable to the driver of a motor vehicle (e.g., must stop at stop signs and red lights, yield to emergency vehicles, etc.), except those provisions which by their nature can not apply. (Ref. Sec. 21200)

EQUIPMENT

Brakes - No person shall operate a bicycle on a roadway unless it is equipped with a brake which will enable the operator to make one wheel skid on dry, level, clean pavement. (Ref. Sec. 21201 a)

Handlebars - No person shall operate on the highway any bicycle equipped with handlebars so raised that the operator must elevate his hands above the level of his shoulders in order to grasp the normal steering grip area. (Ref. Sec. 21201 b)

Bicycle Size - No person shall operate upon any highway a bicycle which is of such a size as to prevent the operator from safely stopping the bicycle, supporting it in an upright position with at least one foot on the ground, and restarting it in a safe manner. (Ref. Sec. 21201 c)

Lights and Reflectors - Every bicycle operated upon any highway during darkness shall be equipped (1) with a lamp emitting a white light which, while the bicycle is in motion, illuminated the highway in front of the bicyclist and is visible from a distance of 300 feet in front and from the sides of the bicycle (or a lamp or lamp combination meeting the same requirements may be attached to the operator); (2) with a red reflector of a type approved by the Department of Motor Vehicles on the rear which shall be visible from a distance of 500 feet to the rear when directly in front of lawful upper beams of headlamps on a motor vehicle; in front of lawful upper beams of headlamps on a motor vehicle; (3) with white or yellow reflector, of a type approved by the Department on each pedal visible from the front and rear of the bicycle from a distance of 200 feet; and (4) with a white or yellow reflector on each side forward of the center of the bicycle, and with a white or red reflector on each side to the rear of the center of the bicycle, except that bicycles which are equipped with reflectorized tires on the front and rear need not be equipped with these side reflectors. (Ref. Sec. 21201d, e)

RULES OF THE ROAD

Two- Way Streets- Any person operating a bicycle upon a roadway at a speed less than the normal speed of traffic moving in the same direction at such time shall ride as close as practicable to the righthand curb or edge of the roadway except under any of the following situations:
1. When overtaking and passing another bicycle or motor vehicle proceeding in the same direction.
2. When preparing for a left turn at an intersection or into a private road or driveway.
3. When reasonably necessary to avoid conditions (including but not limited to fixed or moving objects, vehicles, bicycles, pedestrians, animals, surface hazards, or substandard width lanes) that make it unsafe to continue along the right hand curb or edge. For purposes of this section, a "substandard width lane" is a lane that is too narrow for a bicycle and a vehicle to travel safely side by side within the land. (Ref. Sec. 21202 a)

One-Way Streets - Any person operating a bicycle upon a roadway of a highway, which highway carries traffic in one direction only and has two or more marked traffic lanes, may ride as near as the left hand curb or edge of such roadway as practicable. (Ref. Sec. 21202 b)

Bicycle Lanes - Whenever a bicycle has been established on a roadway, any person operating a bicycle upon the roadway at a speed less than the normal speed of traffic moving in the same direction shall ride within the bicycle lane, except that such persons may move out of the lane under any of the following situations:
1. When overtaking and passing another bicycle, vehicle or pedestrian within the lane or about to enter the lane if such overtaking and passing cannot be done safely within the lane.
2. When preparing for a left turn at an intersection or into a private road or driveway.
3. When reasonably necessary to leave the bicycle lane to avoid debris or other hazardous conditions. (Ref. Sec. 21208 a)
No person operating a bicyle shall leave a bicyle lane until the movement can be made with reasonably safety and then only after giving an appropriate signal in the event that any vehicle may be affected by the movement. (Ref. Sec. 21208 b)

Hitching Rides - No person riding upon a bicycle shall attach the bicycle or himself to any street car or vehicle on the roadway. (Ref. Sec. 21203)

Riding on Seats - No person operating a bicycle upon a highway shall ride other than upon or astride a permanent and regular attached seat. (Ref. Sec. 21204 a)

No operator shall allow a person riding as a passenger, and no person shall ride as a passenger, on a bicycle upon a highway other than upon or astride a separate attached seat. If the passenger is a minor weighing 40 pounds or less, the seat shall have adequate provision for retaining the minor in place and for protection the minor from the moving parts of the bicycle. (Ref. Sec. 21204 b)

Carrying Articles - No person operating a bicycle shall carry any package, bundle or article which prevents the operator from keeping at least one hand upon the handlebars. (Ref. Sec. 21205) ·

Hand Signals - All required signals given by hand and arm shall be given in the following manner:
1. Left turn - hand and arm extended horizontally beyond the side of the bicycle.
2. Right turn - left hand and arm extended upward beyond the side of the bicycle or right hand and arm extended horizontally to right side of the bicycle.
3. Stop or sudden decrease of speed signal — hand and arm extended downward beyond the side of the vehicle. (Ref. Sec. 22111)

Parking - No person shall leave a bicycle on its side on any sidewalk, or shall park a bicycle on a sidewalk in any other position, so that there is not an adequate path for pedestrian traffic. (Ref. Sec. 21210)

MARIN COUNTY ORDINANCE

Chapter 13.24 (Applicable in unincorporated areas only)

BICYCLES

Section 13.24.010 - Definitions

A. Bicycle. The term "bicycle" shall mean any device upon which any person may ride, propelled exclusively by human power, through a belt, chain or gears, and having either two or three wheels of at least 20 inches in diameter in a tandem or tricycle arrangement.
B. Motorized Bicycle. A "motorized bicycle" is a two-wheeled or three-wheeled device having fully operative pedals for propulsion by human power, or having no pedals if powered solely by electrical energy, and an automatic transmission and a motor which produces less than 2 gross brake horsepower and is capable of propelling the device at a maximum speed of not more than 30 miles per hour on level ground.

Section 13.24.030 - Any person operating a bicycle or motorized bicycle within the County of Marin shall comply with all provisions of the California Vehicle Code which pertain to bicycles and motorized bicycles.

Section 13.24.030 - Bicycles Prohibited on Sidewalk.
A. No person shall ride a bicycle upon the sidewalk within a business district which is zoned for that purpose.
B. No person 14 or more years of age shall ride a bicycle on any sidewalk in any district.

Section 13.24.040 - Multipurpose Recreational Trails. Any person operating a bicycle on a multipurpose recreational trail shall yield the right of way to pedestrians and horses.

Section 13.24.050 - Use of trails.
A. It shall be unlawful for any person to operate, ride propel, or park a motorized bicycle on any county multipurpose recreational trail or bicycle trail, except the bike paths from:
1. Gate Six in Sausalito to the former County Heliport;
2. The west shoulder of Highway 101 from
Lincoln Avenue to Los Ranchito Road;
3. The west shoulder of Highway 101 from Miller Creek Road to Alameda Del Prado; and
4. Highway 37 to Hamilton Drive.
B. Any motorized bicycle which is authorized to be operated on a multipurpose recreational trail or bicycle trail shall not exceed a maximum speed of fifteen miles per hour on said trail.

NOTES